You Know You're a
REPUBLICAN
DEMOCRAT
If...

D0071768

FRANK BENJAMIN

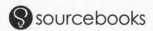

Published by Sourcebooks, Inc.
P.O. Box 4410, Naperville, Illinois 60567-4410
(630) 961-3900
Fax: (630) 961-2168
www.sourcebooks.com

Library of Congress Cataloging-in-Publication Data

Benjamin, Frank.
  You know you're a Republican/Democrat if— / Frank Benjamin. — 3rd edition.
    pages cm
  (trade paper : alk. paper) 1. Republican Party (U.S. : 1854–)—Humor. 2. Democratic Party (U.S.)—Humor. I. Title.
  PN6231.P6B39 2016
  818'.602—dc23
                           2015035059

Printed and bound in the United States of America.

VP 10 9 8 7 6 5 4 3 2

You Know You're a
REPUBLICAN If...

You still believe in mom, apple pie, and the American Way.

You Know You're a
DEMOCRAT If...

You also believe in mom, apple pie, and the American Way, as long as that includes having two moms, the pie is gluten-free, and "American Way" refers to tribal practices of Native Americans.

You Know You're a
REPUBLICAN If...

You start off on third base and think you've hit a triple.

You Know You're a
DEMOCRAT If...

You hit a single but believe
you deserve a triple because
the other team got one.

You Know You're a
REPUBLICAN If...

You think Russian president Vladimir Putin has become an aggressive dictator, an egomaniac, and an amazingly popular leader. You think he should write a management book.

You Know You're a
DEMOCRAT If...

You think Putin is a big, bad bully. He scares you and confuses you. He probably had a rough childhood and could use a really good therapist.

You Know You're a
REPUBLICAN If...

You believe the U.S. Constitution clearly supports strip mining.

You Know You're a
DEMOCRAT If...

You believe the U.S. Constitution clearly supports strippers.

You Know You're a
REPUBLICAN If...

You can't stand your gay uncle,
but you invite him to your son's
wedding because he's rich.

You Know You're a
DEMOCRAT If...

You can't stand your rich uncle, but you invite him to your daughter's graduation party because he's gay.

You Know You're a
REPUBLICAN If...

You can't fathom that Abraham
Lincoln was actually a Republican!

You Know You're a
DEMOCRAT If...

You can't fathom that Abraham Lincoln was actually a Republican!

You Know You're a
REPUBLICAN If...

The song "Amazing Grace" has been tainted forever for you because Obama sang it in South Carolina.

You Know You're a
DEMOCRAT If...

You haven't been to church in twenty years but now sing "Amazing Grace" in the shower every morning.

You Know You're a
REPUBLICAN If...

You're certain Santa Claus is a
Republican. He's overweight, he
smokes a pipe, he's old-fashioned,
and his elves work without a union
contract for less than minimum wage.

You Know You're a
DEMOCRAT If...

You're certain Santa Claus is a Democrat. He gives rather than takes, and he cares if you've been good or not. But you shouldn't call him overweight; he's just dietarily challenged. And you're sure he doesn't inhale.

You Know You're a
REPUBLICAN If...

Your hunting dog wears a Confederate flag bandanna around his neck.

You Know You're a
DEMOCRAT If...

You wouldn't even pick
up your dog's poop with a
Confederate flag bandanna.

You Know You're a
REPUBLICAN If...

You're a firm believer
in the righteousness of
"enlightened self-interest."

You Know You're a
DEMOCRAT If...

You believe an "enlightened
Republican" is an oxymoron.

You Know You're a
REPUBLICAN If...

Your high school class voted you "Most Likely to Wear Pinstripes or Prison Stripes."

You Know You're a
DEMOCRAT If...

Your high school voted you "Most
Likely to Personally Solve World
Hunger"—and you didn't
get the joke.

You Know You're a
REPUBLICAN If...

You own a thirty-foot bullet speedboat named *Just Desserts*.

You Know You're a
DEMOCRAT If...

You own a thirty-foot sailboat named *Guilty Pleasure*.

You Know You're a
REPUBLICAN If...

You have a tender spot in your heart for corporate tax attorneys.

You Know You're a
DEMOCRAT If...

You have a tender spot in your heart
for product liability trial lawyers.

You Know You're a
REPUBLICAN If...

You favor free speech, except
for burning the flag or criticizing
U.S. military spending.

You Know You're a
DEMOCRAT If...

You favor free speech, except for ugly words about minorities, gays, immigrants, the disabled, the obese, the homeless, children, women, or men (excluding Republicans).

You Know You're a
REPUBLICAN If...

You've watched the movie *Saving Private Ryan* six times, and every time you cried at the end.

You Know You're a
DEMOCRAT If...

You cried watching *Bambi* as a kid, and you've been in therapy ever since.

You Know You're a
REPUBLICAN If...

You ran for county dogcatcher on a platform of smaller government, lower taxes, respect for the flag, and withdrawing from the UN.

You Know You're a
DEMOCRAT If...

You ran for county dogcatcher so
you could let the dogs go free.

You Know You're a
REPUBLICAN If...

You're a political history buff and you're convinced John Kennedy "stole" the 1960 presidential election because of vote tampering by Chicago's Mayor Daley.

You Know You're a
DEMOCRAT If...

You think George W. Bush "stole" the 2000 presidential election because of vote tampering by the U.S. Supreme Court.

You Know You're a
REPUBLICAN If...

You're afraid of the IRS.

You Know You're a
DEMOCRAT If...

You're afraid of the FBI.

You Know You're a
REPUBLICAN If...

Your fourteen Facebook friends are bankers, stockbrokers, accountants, and your adult children—all of whom want to curry favor with you. You ignore them all.

You Know You're a
DEMOCRAT If...

Your 4,822 Facebook friends are mostly
strangers who post their innermost
angsts, passions, motivational
sayings, and darling photos of cats.
You're enthralled by them all.

You Know You're a
REPUBLICAN If...

You think public education is broken and doesn't deserve more money, and you send your children to an expensive private school.

You Know You're a
DEMOCRAT If...

You think public education is the backbone of America, but it just needs more money, and you send your children to an expensive private school.

You Know You're a
REPUBLICAN If...

You think "Clinton" is a
four-letter word.

You Know You're a
DEMOCRAT If...

You think "Bush" is a four-letter word. Hey, wait a minute! It is!

You Know You're a
REPUBLICAN If...

You prove your racial sensitivity by saying *gracias* to your gardener.

You Know You're a
DEMOCRAT If...

You're strongly committed to racial equality even if you personally don't have any friends of a different race.

You Know You're a
REPUBLICAN If...

You have a picture of yourself shaking hands with Ronald Reagan hanging on your office wall.

You Know You're a
DEMOCRAT If...

You have a picture of Ronald Reagan hanging in the middle of your dartboard.

You Know You're a
REPUBLICAN If...

You've thought about becoming a Libertarian, but you have trouble with their philosophical support of prostitution, gay marriage, and unhindered personal freedom.

You Know You're a
DEMOCRAT If...

You've thought about becoming a
Libertarian, but you have trouble
with their support of free trade,
school vouchers, and guns.

You Know You're a
REPUBLICAN If...

Your favorite initials are
NRA, RNC, FOX, and WSJ.

You Know You're a
DEMOCRAT If...

Your favorite initials are
MLK, JFK, AFL-CIO, and PBS.

You Know You're a
REPUBLICAN If...

At some point in your life you won a skeet shooting trophy, a polo playing trophy, or a trophy wife.

You Know You're a DEMOCRAT If...

You received the Good Conduct Award in grade school.

You Know You're a
REPUBLICAN If...

Your excuse for buying a gas-guzzling SUV is, "Mind your own damn business."

You Know You're a
DEMOCRAT If...

Your excuse for buying a gas-guzzling SUV is, "Well, umm, I plan to deliver Meals on Wheels to hungry endangered species in the wilderness."

You Know You're a
REPUBLICAN If...

You have a good stock portfolio,
but your conscience is nagging
you about your big investment
in tobacco companies.

You Know You're a
DEMOCRAT If...

You have a clear conscience,
but you really miss the days
when smoking was fun.

You Know You're a
REPUBLICAN If...

You wouldn't mind if
the Commonwealth of
Massachusetts seceded
from the Union.

You Know You're a
DEMOCRAT If...

You wish the Republic of Texas
had never become a state.

You Know You're a
REPUBLICAN If...

You give a beggar your business card, invite him to come apply for a job, and walk away feeling smug and self-righteous.

You Know You're a
DEMOCRAT If...

You give a beggar a dollar
and walk away worrying
he'll spend it on booze.

You Know You're a
REPUBLICAN If...

You're an evangelical Christian or look favorably upon evangelicals because they vote Republican.

You Know You're a
DEMOCRAT If...

Evangelical Christians make you nervous. You think they all want to convert you to their religion or, worse, to Republicanism.

You Know You're a
REPUBLICAN If...

You think Bruce (Caitlyn) Jenner is a transsexual freak or scam artist, but you respect his (her) right to get rich off it.

You Know You're a
DEMOCRAT If...

You're so proud that Caitlyn (Bruce) Jenner is trying to find her (his) real self, but you wish she (he) wasn't related to those money-grubbing Kardashians.

You Know You're a
REPUBLICAN If...

You support an increase in the U.S. military budget, especially for the base in your congressional district.

You Know You're a
DEMOCRAT If...

You want to slash the U.S. military budget, as long as they don't touch the base in your congressional district.

You Know You're a
REPUBLICAN If...

You buy a big gas-guzzling SUV, thus sending American dollars to buy oil from Middle East countries where everyone hates America.

You Know You're a
DEMOCRAT If...

You buy a modest Asian or European car, thus sending American jobs to countries where everyone hates America.

You Know You're a
REPUBLICAN If...

You disagree that all public buildings
need to be wheelchair accessible, but
you believe public lands should
be open to anyone with an oil
rig, an ATV, or a shotgun.

You Know You're a
DEMOCRAT If...

You think every building, including the top of the Washington Monument, should be accessible using a wheelchair or Seeing Eye dog, but public wilderness areas should be open only to those who can hike ten miles in and out.

You Know You're a
REPUBLICAN If...

You're quietly disappointed that the Iraq war turned into such a quagmire, but you're sure we'll get it right when we invade Iran.

You Know You're a
DEMOCRAT If...

You're opposed to any military intervention in the sovereign affairs of other countries, unless Hillary tells you it's the right thing to do.

You Know You're a
REPUBLICAN If...

You feel you must hide your
secret passion for reading
the *New York Times*.

You Know You're a
DEMOCRAT If...

You feel you must hide your secret passion for watching stock car racing.

You Know You're a
REPUBLICAN If...

You philosophically oppose
government welfare plans,
but you cash your Social
Security checks religiously.

You Know You're a
DEMOCRAT If...

You're philosophically appalled by corporate America's emphasis on profits, but you were sure ticked off when your retirement investments tanked.

You Know You're a REPUBLICAN If...

You're dealt great cards at poker, win big, gloat obnoxiously, but agree to buy the beer at the next game.

You Know You're a
DEMOCRAT If...

You beat your tennis partner soundly two games in a row, feel guilty, call it luck, and suggest you play three out of five.

You Know You're a
REPUBLICAN If...

You prefer your steaks
rare and your jokes raw.

You Know You're a
DEMOCRAT If...

You prefer your vegetables raw, you don't eat meat, and you don't tell jokes...because jokes are about victimhood, and you don't want any part in that—unless the jokes are about Republicans.

You Know You're a
REPUBLICAN If...

You like expensive toys and bought a drone so you can scope out potential land purchases, spot elk easier when hunting, and, most importantly, spy on your hot neighbor when she sunbathes.

You Know You're a
DEMOCRAT If...

After first checking to make sure
no birds would be hurt, you bought
a drone to photograph the illegal
pollution at the chemical plant,
secretly surveil animal abuse at the
inhumane chicken farm, and spy on
your hot neighbor when she sunbathes.

You Know You're a
REPUBLICAN If...

You're very proud of your housekeeper's son, who is serving in the U.S. military.

You Know You're a
DEMOCRAT If...

You don't personally know anyone
who is serving in the U.S. military.

You Know You're a
REPUBLICAN If...

You've never seen a government social services program that you thought justified raising your taxes.

You Know You're a
DEMOCRAT If...

You've never seen a social services program that you weren't willing to spend other taxpayers' money on.

You Know You're a
REPUBLICAN If...

Your daughter's "coming out" party gets special mention in the society page of the newspaper.

You Know You're a DEMOCRAT If...

Your son's "coming out" party is written up in the Gay Alliance newsletter.

You Know You're a
REPUBLICAN If...

You firmly believe in personal privacy in the bedroom, but you try not to think about same-sex coupling.

You Know You're a
DEMOCRAT If...

You firmly believe in personal privacy
in the bedroom, but the thought
of two Republicans procreating
sends shivers down your spine.

You Know You're a
REPUBLICAN If...

You want to visit Cuba now and see the old American cars from the 1950s still being driven because it's the closest you'll ever get to "restoring America to the way it was."

You Know You're a
DEMOCRAT If...

You want to visit Cuba too. You want to see for yourself that the Castro brothers weren't really so bad after all. Were they?

You Know You're a
REPUBLICAN If...

You're totally baffled by the Israeli-Palestinian conflict, but you believe the Democrats messed it up.

You Know You're a
DEMOCRAT If...

You're totally flummoxed
by the Israeli-Palestinian
conflict, but you're certain the
Republicans messed it up first.

You Know You're a
REPUBLICAN If...

You own two cows.
Your neighbor has none.
He feels cheated; he wants
one of your cows.
So?

You Know You're a
DEMOCRAT If...

You own two cows.

Your neighbor has none.

He doesn't want a cow; he wants a pig.

You insist the government give
him a cow; pigs are bad for you.

You still have two cows.

You are happy.

You Know You're a
REPUBLICAN If...

You liked high school.
You studied hard enough to get into
the college you wanted to attend.
You had a girlfriend with nice hair.
Life was good.

You Know You're a
DEMOCRAT If...

You couldn't wait to get
out of high school.

You either were a feminist or dated one.

You studied your butt off.

You joined the debate team or the
school paper or, better yet, both.

You wore black.

You Know You're a
REPUBLICAN If...

You got a B on your
accounting midterm.

Your fraternity just had a rockin'
Fiesta Night with margaritas and
great Mexican food, and you met
a hot chick with nice hair.

Your favorite T-shirt reads "IMHOT4U."

College is even better than high school!

You Know You're a
DEMOCRAT If...

You got a B on your sociology essay,
"Why the Term 'Mexican Food'
Is Racist and Demeaning."
You will need to skip the Greenpeace
rally to revise it and on Monday beg
the professor to let you resubmit it.
Your favorite T-shirt reads "Off Limits!"
College is even more stressful
than high school!

You Know You're a
REPUBLICAN If...

You paid $1,000 to stuff the
head of the trophy buck you
shot. You share the venison
with your business partner.

You Know You're a
DEMOCRAT If...

You paid $1,000 for a guided trout fishing excursion that was, of course, strictly catch and release.

You Know You're a REPUBLICAN If...

There are three people in your household and you own four vehicles—not counting the two ATVs.

You Know You're a
DEMOCRAT If...

The three cars you and your wife own all get good gas mileage.

You Know You're a
REPUBLICAN If...

You admit it's time we let
hardworking American entrepreneurs
in Colorado get rich selling marijuana.

You Know You're a
DEMOCRAT If...

You're thinking, "Dude! I didn't know I was an entrepurr-whatever. I thought I was just a pothead!"

You Know You're a
REPUBLICAN If...

You're infuriated by the shoddy shape of America's infrastructure. You insist we fix our crumbling roads, bridges, power grid, and airports to remain competitive. You refuse to pay for any of it.

You Know You're a
DEMOCRAT If...

You're saddened by the terrible condition of America's infrastructure. You believe we need to commit tax dollars to fixing it... as soon as we solve global warming.

You Know You're a
REPUBLICAN If...

You're furious about the severe
drought because you can't
fill your swimming pool.

You Know You're a
DEMOCRAT If...

You're incensed that corporate agribusinesses are allocated most of the water and you can't water the vegetables in your neighborhood co-op garden.

You Know You're a
REPUBLICAN If...

Your smartphone has apps for the *Wall Street Journal*, Fox News, TeaParty.net, ConcealedCarry.com, and Candy Crush.

You Know You're a
DEMOCRAT If...

Your smartphone has apps for the *New York Times*, NPR, *New Republic*, *Mother Jones*, *Slate*, MoveOn.org, and Candy Crush.

You Know You're a
REPUBLICAN If...

Your vanity license plate
reads "IMB4U."

You Know You're a
DEMOCRAT If...

Your vanity license plate
reads "LUVGOV."

You Know You're a
REPUBLICAN If...

Free enterprise is in your blood, but
it rankles you that Bill and Hillary
earn outrageous speaking fees.

You Know You're a
DEMOCRAT If...

It sort of bothers you that the Clintons make obscene speaking fees, but you're pleased George Bush can only get a fraction as much.

You Know You're a
REPUBLICAN If...

You have a home aquarium. The big fish kills the little fish. So you get another big fish. They fight constantly. "Animals are like that," you think.

You Know You're a
DEMOCRAT If...

You own a home aquarium. The big fish kills the little fish. You hold a funeral for the little fish. You are at a loss for what to do. You give away the big fish. You put the empty aquarium in the attic. "Whew, no more fighting," you think.

You Know You're a
REPUBLICAN If...

When you were a teenager, you worked after school to save money. You bought a used Ford pickup. Your friend's dad bought her a new Mustang. You were envious. You wanted to swap dads.

You Know You're a
DEMOCRAT If...

Your dad bought you a cute new Mustang. You felt guilty. You felt guilty every day. You did nothing.

You Know You're a
REPUBLICAN If...

You think government agencies
should be run like businesses,
with management free to fire
incompetent employees at will.

You Know You're a
DEMOCRAT If...

You think businesses should be run like government agencies, with workers protected from firing no matter how incompetent.

You Know You're a
REPUBLICAN If...

You don't pray much yourself,
but you zealously defend the
idea of prayer in schools.

You Know You're a
DEMOCRAT If...

You insist upon a strict separation of church and state, unless it threatens your daughter's federal financial aid to Notre Dame.

You Know You're a
REPUBLICAN If...

You generally respect police chiefs, but you can't understand why they support limitations on assault weapons.

You Know You're a
DEMOCRAT If...

You distrust the police and want
to take their guns away too.

You Know You're a
REPUBLICAN If...

You oppose government-subsidized transit, but you expect the public works department to fix that pothole on your street...now!

You Know You're a
DEMOCRAT If...

You support spending millions on taxpayer-subsidized mass transit used by a tiny fraction of the populace while thousands of fellow taxpayers are stuck in traffic jams on overcrowded highways wasting vast amounts of gas.

You Know You're a
REPUBLICAN If...

You thank God every day for the gifts He has bestowed upon you and your family, especially your tax-free inheritance.

You Know You're a
DEMOCRAT If...

You thank God every day for the strength She gives you to fight for truth, justice, and punitive damage awards.

You Know You're a
REPUBLICAN If...

Your dog gets better health care
than your housekeeper.

You Know You're a
DEMOCRAT If...

Regardless of the cost, you support free, unlimited, universal health care including coverage for birth control, maternity care, hearing aids, abortion, prosthetics, orthodontics, dental floss, teeth whitening, Botox injections, earwax removal, and, oh yeah, pet care too.

You Know You're a
REPUBLICAN If...

You thought all your college
professors were flaming liberals.

You Know You're a
DEMOCRAT If...

You *are* a college professor.

You Know You're a
REPUBLICAN If...

You think every Democrat
is a closet Communist.

You Know You're a
DEMOCRAT If...

You think every Republican
is closeted.

You Know You're a
REPUBLICAN If...

Drought be damned, you equipped your
bathroom shower with a wonderful
gushing waterfall showerhead, and
you don't care if neighbors think
you're insensitive about conserving
water. You're willing to pay for
all the water you consume.

You Know You're a
DEMOCRAT If...

You only shower twice a week and you've equipped your home with low-volume toilets, a high-efficiency hot water heater, and a "green" clothes dryer. But please don't raise the water rates! You've already blown a fortune being sensitive.

You Know You're a
REPUBLICAN If...

You've learned that the secret to a
youthful appearance is a good personal
trainer and a great plastic surgeon.

You Know You're a
DEMOCRAT If...

You've learned that the secret to a youthful appearance is yoga, coconut water, and a *quiet* plastic surgeon.

You Know You're a
REPUBLICAN If...

You think Sean Hannity, Lauren Green, and Rush Limbaugh are intellectual powerhouses, and you've learned many insights from their wisdom.

You Know You're a
DEMOCRAT If...

Everything you know about politics you learned from Jon Stewart, Stephen Colbert, and Bill Maher.

You Know You're a
REPUBLICAN If...

You and your third spouse vehemently oppose same-sex marriage as an insult to the sacred institution of matrimony.

You Know You're a
DEMOCRAT If...

You firmly believe marriage should be allowed between consenting adults of the same species—although you do know some women who are madly in love with their cats and, well...

You Know You're a
REPUBLICAN If...

You believe human cloning is
morally objectionable unless,
of course, they figure out how
to resurrect Ronald Reagan.

You Know You're a
DEMOCRAT If...

You think it would be cool to clone
Bill Clinton, minus a few body parts.

You Know You're a
REPUBLICAN If...

You're convinced the federal
government wants to foist the
Common Core education standards
on the states as part of a communist-
like effort to brainwash the American
people. You've never read the
standards yourself, of course.

You Know You're a
DEMOCRAT If...

You know that the states, not the federal government, created the Common Core standards, which will elevate K–12 education to a higher level. You've never read the standards yourself, of course.

You Know You're a
REPUBLICAN If...

On Cinco de Mayo, you give your maid the day off, even though you have no idea what the holiday celebrates.

You Know You're a
DEMOCRAT If...

On Cinco de Mayo, your family celebrates more than on the Fourth of July, even though it's a Mexican holiday.

You Know You're a
REPUBLICAN If...

You blame your obesity on your hectic schedule and your unrestricted expense account.

You Know You're a
DEMOCRAT If...

You blame your obesity on every fast-food restaurant you've ever visited, your neighborhood grocery store, all the cookie manufacturers, and your mother—and you're gonna sue 'em all!

You Know You're a
REPUBLICAN If...

You resent Hollywood celebrities who write big checks and publicly support Democratic candidates. Big checks are supposed to come from billionaire business moguls who *quietly* support Republican candidates.

You Know You're a
DEMOCRAT If...

You're thankful that hundreds of thousands of supporters send small checks to support Democratic candidates, along with those big checks from Hollywood celebrities whose busy red carpet schedules keep them from voting.

You Know You're a
REPUBLICAN If...

You want to stem the tide of illegal immigrants getting into the U.S. But then again, somebody's got to mow your lawn.

You Know You're a
DEMOCRAT If...

You sympathize with undocumented workers ("illegal immigrants" sounds so, well, harsh), but the unions want the borders closed and... Oh, shoot, you're just so confused!

You Know You're a
REPUBLICAN If...

Your minister says he will pray for your soul if you pay for a new meeting hall.

You Know You're a
DEMOCRAT If...

Your minister says she knows your soul is doing just fine, but could you please bake some cookies to help raise money for a new meeting hall.

You Know You're a
REPUBLICAN If...

Your idea of "compassionate conservatism" means giving your employees praise instead of a raise.

You Know You're a
DEMOCRAT If...

Your idea of "liberalism" means spending other people's money liberally on causes you support.

You Know You're a
REPUBLICAN If...

Your car displays a bumper sticker saying, "The Lord giveth and the Democrats taketh away."

You Know You're a
DEMOCRAT If...

Your bumper sticker says, "The Lord giveth and the Republicans keepeth. Until now."

You Know You're a
REPUBLICAN If...

You visited Disney World as a kid, and the Magic Kingdom castle reminded you of your family's summer home.

You Know You're a
DEMOCRAT If...

You visited Disney World as a kid and thought the depiction of the animatronic bears was insensitive and specieist.

You Know You're a
REPUBLICAN If...

You think more criminals should be locked up for as long as possible, and new jails to hold them can be built with money saved by opening schools to competition...or cutting back on food stamps...or something like that, surely!

You Know You're a
DEMOCRAT If...

You think criminals had rough childhoods and could use a little TLC.

You Know You're a
REPUBLICAN If...

Your Twitter handle is @luvcash.

You Know You're a
DEMOCRAT If...

Your Twitter handle is @luvluv.

You Know You're a
REPUBLICAN If...

You're 100 percent certain that the one scientist in a thousand who debunks global warming is right.

You Know You're a
DEMOCRAT If...

You're 100 percent certain that global warming is imminent and you want everyone to ride the bus (as long as the bus runs on electricity or compressed natural gas or biodiesel or recycled chicken poop).

You Know You're a
REPUBLICAN If...

You won three Texas beauty contests when you were a teenager, and by God, you're going to buy your teenage daughter those double-D breast implants she needs to win a few too.

You Know You're a
DEMOCRAT If...

You would never buy breast implants for your daughter, unless she was having self-esteem issues, and if that's the case, you really think health insurance should pay for them. (Will they help her get into Berkeley?)

You Know You're a
REPUBLICAN If...

Your father owned a baseball team.

You Know You're a
DEMOCRAT If...

Your father helped unionize the
stadium concessionaires.

You Know You're a
REPUBLICAN If...

When your daughter's soccer team came in dead last at the tournament but still gave every player a trophy just for "showing up," you sneered and tossed the trophy in the trash, and your daughter cried.

You Know You're a
DEMOCRAT If...

When your daughter's soccer team won the tournament and every player got a trophy saying "First Place," you felt guilty and hid the trophy, and your daughter cried.

You Know You're a
REPUBLICAN If...

You've accepted that global warming is real and that the polar ice packs are melting at an alarming rate, but you don't believe we should panic and recklessly raise taxes to fix it. You have, however, invested in future beachfront property—twenty miles inland.

You Know You're a
DEMOCRAT If...

For a long time now you've known that: The sky is falling! The sky is falling! No, wait. The sky is cooking! The sky is cooking!

You Know You're a
REPUBLICAN If...

You're a huge fan of government
subsidies for wind turbines
to generate electricity, as
long as you own them.

You Know You're a
DEMOCRAT If...

You're an even bigger fan of subsidies for wind turbines, as long as Republicans don't own them.

You Know You're a
REPUBLICAN If...

You've conveniently forgotten that the Environmental Protection Agency was created during the Nixon administration.

You Know You're a
DEMOCRAT If...

You still can't believe the EPA was created during the Nixon administration.

You Know You're a
REPUBLICAN If...

You still have some vague sense
that Congress, not the executive
branch, is supposed to come up
with *new* legislation, but you
really just want to repeal anything
accomplished by Obama.

You Know You're a
DEMOCRAT If...

You have no idea what Congress is supposed to do anymore, but you're certainly glad the Obama administration found ways to get stuff done by going around it.

You Know You're a
REPUBLICAN If...

You try to avoid too much MSG
in the Chinese food you eat.

You Know You're a
DEMOCRAT If...

You think the MSG in Chinese food should be regulated by the FDA, the Department of Agriculture, the Center for Disease Control, the FBI, the Defense Department, and Oprah.

You Know You're a
REPUBLICAN If...

You proudly shop at Walmart.

You Know You're a
DEMOCRAT If...

Because of Walmart's terrible reputation for low-wage labor, sexism, and manufacturing its products at overseas sweatshops, you only shop at Walmart late at night when no one will recognize you.

You Know You're a
REPUBLICAN If...

You visit Vegas. You win big at the craps table the first night. You're amazed at your luck. You lose it all and more the next night. You're mad you didn't quit when you were ahead. You plan to come back.

You Know You're a
DEMOCRAT If...

You visit Vegas. You win big at craps the first night. You're proud of your betting skills. You lose it all and more the next night. You blame loaded dice, the crooked casino, the mafia, and, for good measure, Republicans. You say you won't come back.

You Know You're a
REPUBLICAN If...

Your parents wanted you to go to college, join the Peace Corps, and become a teacher. Instead you joined a fraternity and Young Republicans and became an investment banker.

You Know You're a
DEMOCRAT If...

Your parents wanted you to go to college, join the Peace Corps, and become a teacher. You did.

You Know You're a
REPUBLICAN If...

Sure, you'd really like to be concerned about the little guy, but you're terrified the government will tax the rich more and stifle economic growth.

You Know You're a
DEMOCRAT If...

You don't worry much about
economic growth as long as
we tax the rich more.

You Know You're a
REPUBLICAN If...

Someone calling you a
"liberal" makes you mad.

You Know You're a
DEMOCRAT If...

Someone calling you a
"liberal" makes you squirm.

You Know You're a
REPUBLICAN If...

If you were a college president, you'd demand that professors work a forty-hour week, that true freedom of speech includes criticism of the faculty and of other students, and that students not come to class drunk or stoned.

You Know You're a
DEMOCRAT If...

You *were* a faculty member before you became a college president. You think academic research is the backbone of higher education, that the school should educate the "whole person," although you have no clue what that means, and that free speech is important if it doesn't hurt anyone's self-esteem.

You Know You're a
REPUBLICAN If...

You'd love to put "Christ" back into Christmas, but baby Jesus dolls don't sell nearly as well as stuffed Santas and Frostys.

You Know You're a
DEMOCRAT If...

You think it's a racist plot that Frosty the Snowman is always depicted as a white guy.

You Know You're a
REPUBLICAN If...

At one time you were a pole dancer but saw the error of your ways, found God, started wearing stylish but modest clothing, developed a taste for Tiffany jewelry, and joined the Junior League— after you became pregnant by and married one of your rich customers.

You Know You're a DEMOCRAT If...

You *are* a pole dancer.

You Know You're a
REPUBLICAN If...

You love Donald Trump's idea
of building an impregnable wall
between the U.S. and Mexico.

You Know You're a
DEMOCRAT If...

You love the idea of building an impregnable wall around Donald Trump.

You Know You're a
REPUBLICAN If...

You shop at Whole Foods grocery stores because you don't mind paying a little extra for good quality food. But you'd prefer it if the checkout person combed his hair and wore deodorant.

You Know You're a
DEMOCRAT If...

You absolutely must buy your groceries at Whole Foods even if your rent money goes toward organic apples, heirloom tomatoes, and all-natural, hormone-free yogurt. You *are* the checkout person.

You Know You're a
REPUBLICAN If...

The fit band you wear every day keeps track of your heart rate, the steps you've taken, your bank balance, and the temperature at your summer home.

You Know You're a
DEMOCRAT If...

The fit band you wear keeps track
of your heart rate, the steps you've
taken, your happy score, and the
melting rate of the polar ice pack.

You Know You're a
REPUBLICAN If...

You are appalled that *Harper's Weekly* once referred to a Republican president as a "despot, liar, thief, braggart, buffoon, usurper, monster, old scoundrel, perjurer, swindler, tyrant, field-butcher, land-pirate." Especially since it was Lincoln they were writing about.

You Know You're a
DEMOCRAT If...

Your head still hurts trying to grasp that Lincoln was a Republican.

You Know You're a
REPUBLICAN If...

You helped your daughter's private school hold its best fund-raiser ever—by selling foreclosed homes.

You Know You're a
DEMOCRAT If...

You and your former domestic partner, now wife, helped at your daughter's school fund-raiser by baking three huge batches of gluten-free, sugar-free, tasteless cookies.

You Know You're a
REPUBLICAN If...

To show your commitment to the environment, you now own an electric car—a $120,000 red Tesla roadster that can accelerate from 0 to 60 in about three seconds. It makes a great second car.

You Know You're a
DEMOCRAT If...

You ride a really cool red bike.

You Know You're a
REPUBLICAN If...

You bought a Donald Trump wig
and wore it proudly to work.

You Know You're a
DEMOCRAT If...

You wore a Donald Trump wig to a Halloween party to scare your friends...and got beat up by a girl wearing a Che Guevara T-shirt.

You Know You're a
REPUBLICAN If...

You think democracy is messy. To tidy it up a bit, you think restricting voter registration might just do the trick.

You Know You're a
DEMOCRAT If...

You also recognize democracy is messy, but don't mess with voter registration. Besides, if the voters get something wrong, we can always turn to the Supreme Court to tidy it up a bit.

You Know You're a
REPUBLICAN If...

You didn't understand some of the
cynical jokes about Republicans
on the previous pages.

You Know You're a
DEMOCRAT If...

Your feelings were hurt by some of
the mean jokes about Democrats
on the previous pages.

About the Author

Frank Benjamin is the pseudonym of a university vice president who is (a) cautious, (b) cowardly, (c) modest, (d) all of the above, or perhaps (e) just fond of multiple-choice tests. Now working in the bustling arena of online education, Frank enjoys regular contact with business executives and governors of both political stripes, who, he notes graciously, "usually can laugh at themselves." Usually.